Canning, Storing & Preserving Explained

Preserving and Canning Food for Beginners

Food Preservation Techniques, Canning Methods, Tools and Equipment, Common Canning Recipes and More!

By Cynthia Cherry

Copyrights and Trademarks

All rights reserved. No part of this book may be reproduced or transformed in any form or by any means, graphic, electronic, or mechanical, including photocopying, recording, taping, or by any information storage retrieval system, without the written permission of the author.

This publication is Copyright ©2019 NRB Publishing, an imprint. Nevada. All products, graphics, publications, software and services mentioned and recommended in this publication are protected by trademarks. In such instance, all trademarks & copyright belong to the respective owners. For information consult www.NRBpublishing.com

Disclaimer and Legal Notice

This product is not legal, medical, or accounting advice and should not be interpreted in that manner. You need to do your own due-diligence to determine if the content of this product is right for you. While every attempt has been made to verify the information shared in this publication, neither the author, neither publisher, nor the affiliates assume any responsibility for errors, omissions or contrary interpretation of the subject matter herein. Any perceived slights to any specific person(s) or organization(s) are purely unintentional.

We have no control over the nature, content and availability of the web sites listed in this book. The inclusion of any web site links does not necessarily imply a recommendation or endorse the views expressed within them. We take no responsibility for, and will not be liable for, the websites being temporarily unavailable or being removed from the internet.

The accuracy and completeness of information provided herein and opinions stated herein are not guaranteed or warranted to produce any particular results, and the advice and strategies, contained herein may not be suitable for every individual. Neither the author nor the publisher shall be liable for any loss incurred as a consequence of the use and application, directly or indirectly, of any information presented in this work. This publication is designed to provide information in regard to the subject matter covered.

Neither the author nor the publisher assume any responsibility for any errors or omissions, nor do they represent or warrant that the ideas, information, actions, plans, suggestions contained in this book is in all cases accurate. It is the reader's responsibility to find advice before putting anything written in this book into practice. The information in this book is not intended to serve as legal, medical, or accounting advice.

Foreword

People tend to take for granted the ease of getting something out of the refrigerator and just popping it in the microwave to have something to eat. That is one of the things we need to be thankful for now that we live in this age of electronics and technology. In the past, when there was no refrigerator or microwave, one had to remember that food cannot be left out in the heat for a long time—it had to be consumed immediately or preserved in something. Otherwise, eating it would result in stomach flu, food poisoning, and even death.

It is basic right to have access to food. But not everyone enjoys this right and there are a lot of wastage all over the world. Food is vital to health. It is important for life. Therefore, it is important that people understand the importance of properly storing and preserving food to prevent wastage.

In this book, you will find out the many creative ways on how food is being preserved. Food preservation comprises of sets of processes in which food is conserved through various means that ensure food is stored in a safe way to for future consumption. These various creative processes prevent spoilage, avert the growth of poisonous microorganisms in food, and preserve food quality.

Table of Contents

Introduction 1

Chapter One: Importance of Food Preservation and Storage 5

    Importance of Food Preservation 6

    Common Methods of Food Preservation............................ 8

        Drying.. 9

        Chilling and Freezing 10

Chapter Two: Other Methods of Food Preservation 19

    Salting 20

    Sugaring.. 21

    Vacuum Packing 23

    Canning 26

Chapter Three: All About Canning 31

    Before You Start Canning 33

        High Acid Foods + Boiling Water Canner...................... 34

        Low Acid Foods + Pressure Canner 34

    Tools and Equipment 35

    Best Vegetables for Canning... 36

    Best Fruits for Canning 38

    Canning Meat and Poultry 39

    Hot Packed vs. Raw Packed Foods 40

    Practicing Safe Home Canning 42

Hygiene 42

Cooking 44

Storing Canned Products 45

How Canning Preserves Foods.. 46

Does Canning Affect Nutritional Levels of Food? 49

Chapter Four: Canning Techniques 51

Jars and Lids 52

Boiling Water Canning.. 53

Pressure Canning 59

Canned Foods for Special Diets 67

Canning without Sugar.. 67

Canning with less or without Salt 68

Maintaining Color and Flavor in Canned Food 68

Equipment and Methods that are Not Recommended 71

Chapter Five: Pros and Cons of Canning and Consuming Canned Foods.. 73

Consuming Canned Foods 77

Advantages of Consuming Canned Foods 78

Disadvantages of Consuming Canned Foods................ 81

Health Risks 83

Make the Right Choices 84

Chapter Six: Possible Issues with Canned Foods: Causes and Solutions 87

Chapter Seven: Simple Home Canning Recipes 101

   Common Canning Recipes 102

Pesto Sauce 106

Strawberry Basil Jam 120

Holiday Pepper Jelly 126

   Conclusion 130

Photo Credits 133

References 135

Introduction

Take a bag of chips, for instance. Look over the list of ingredients and you will find quite an extensive list of very peculiar chemical names—preservatives that are either natural or synthetic. These preservatives help keep the chips tasting good, prevent spoilage and extend the life of the main ingredient. Open your refrigerator or check your kitchen cupboard and you will find lots of packaged food that have a similar list of ingredients and indications of food's shelf life, longer that what it naturally would have. Check out a bag of dried mangoes or beef jerky.

Introduction

These foods are preserved by drying—the water source is taken out so microorganisms have no chance to multiply and cause food to spoil. Doesn't it make you happy that you can enjoy these kinds of foods without having to worry about spoilage?

Today's generation is lucky to have so many choices available when it comes to preserving and storing food. Years and years of trial and error have allowed people to learn the best and safest methods to lengthen the longevity, preserve the quality, and properly store food. Using the right materials and appropriate food preservation methods, you can do anything! Many options are available: chilling, freezing, drying, salting, sugaring, smoking, vacuum packing, and caning, and researchers are continually studying new methods to preserve and store food.

This means that even if you buy more food than what you need—or if you have a big harvest from your backyard garden—you don't have to waste food! You can apply food preservation and storage techniques! Think about it: you

Introduction

never have to worry about extra tomatoes or bananas that have to go to the bin just because they have become rotten over time. You don't have to feel bad about fruit or vegetable going to waste when you know how to can, salt, pickle or vacuum-pack them. No more rancid smells in your kitchen!

Read on and learn about how you can creatively preserve and store your food and food items. Not only can you enjoy produce and save money, you can share your abundance with your family and friends or you can even earn money out of it!

The purpose of this book is to help you realize the value of preserving and storing food. With the right knowledge, the right materials and by using the appropriate method, you will enjoy food and contribute to society. You can do it—you can start right at your own home.

Introduction

Chapter One: Importance of Food Preservation and Storage

Whether used at home or for commercial purposes, food preservation comprises of various processes that are utilized to prepare food to be stored long-term. Why should you preserve food? All kinds of food start to spoil immediately after being slaughtered or harvested. The deterioration is a result of different microorganisms or chemical changes, hence preservation is necessary to slow down or prevent the spoilage so that food will be safe to eat in the future.

Chapter One: Importance of Food Preservation and Storage

Importance of Food Preservation

Here are the three basic reasons why food must be preserved:

To curtail pathogenic bacteria. Different microorganisms such as salmonella, E. coli, fungi, and other pathogenic bacteria cause food spoilage. These microorganisms multiply on food because of moisture, warmth and time. When food is properly stored using preservation methods, the growth of bacteria is inhibited. Additionally, the oxidation of fats is delayed through preservation methods.

To maintain the best quality of food. Spoilage causes food to lose its quality, and while mild deterioration does not always make food dangerous to eat, it certainly can affect the appearance, texture and taste of the food. The nutritional value of the food can also be lost. Food preservation techniques help keep the quality and nutritional content of food.

Chapter One: Importance of Food Preservation and Storage

To save money. Whether you're at home or you have a food business, waste of food is a waste of money. At home, you should only buy what you need and not more than you can use. It is usually cheaper to buy in bulk and people just don't have time to go to the grocery often they need food so it is necessary for them to stock up.

If you need to buy more than what you can readily use, then you should learn safe food preservation techniques so that you won't have to throw spoiled fruit, vegetables, meat and other food products. This will save you a lot of money. Studies show that in the United States alone, 40% of food is wasted. That's almost half. Can you imagine that other places in the world don't even have food and it is being wasted in other parts of the same world because people don't appreciate it or don't know how to properly store it? Think of all the $$$ wasted. It is time to cut back on waste of food and money.

It is good to learn food preservation techniques not only to save money and to ensure the safety and quality of your food items, but also to gain sense of satisfaction when

Chapter One: Importance of Food Preservation and Storage

you apply said methods. Knowing that you were able to preserve and store food items properly and safely will give also you a feeling of pride and accomplishment.

This book aims to help you understand the best practices of preserving and storing food as well as risks concerning food hygiene. When you gain understanding, you will be empowered to put this knowledge to practice which will not only benefit you but others as well.

Common Methods of Food Preservation

There are many methods of preserving and storing food from simple practices of chilling to complex techniques like canning. There is a wide range of creative options that are available for you to use at home or for commercial purposes. When you learn and practice the best food preservation methods, you will reduce waste, enjoy the quality of your food better, and even increase your profit (if you are selling food).

Chapter One: Importance of Food Preservation and Storage

Following are brief descriptions of the most common food presentation methods known to man:

Drying

The oldest method of food preservation, drying has been done in the Middle Eastern and Asian regions since 12000 BC! Water is removed from food through different methods of evaporation such as sun drying, air drying, wind drying and smoking. Because food is dehydrated, there is no chance for yeasts, mod, bacteria and other microorganisms to thrive.

Today, there are more modern means of drying such as freeze-drying through the use of commercial food dehydrators, as well as the use of household ovens, drum dryers, shelf dryers, and bed dryers. Spray drying, infrared radiation drying, combined thermal hybrid drying and microwave-vacuum drying are also used for commercial purposes. The processes are usually faster than traditional evaporation methods.

Chapter One: Importance of Food Preservation and Storage

Different kinds of foods can be preserved through dehydration or drying such as meat, fish, fruits and vegetables. Dried meat and dried fish have been around for centuries enjoyed both as traditional food and delicacy. Fruits that are dried have sweeter tastes and longer shelf-life. But they often change their form and can be used differently. For instance, grapes become raisins and plums become prunes. Other fruits can be used in recipes, rehydrated or eaten as they are dried, such as dates and figs. Onion, garlic and edible mushrooms are often dried to be utilized as seasonings. Other vegetables that are dried are used as food by hunters, military men and backpackers.

Chilling and Freezing

In the past, chilling was a luxury. Throughout olden times, different civilizations have used snow or ice to preserve food. Not every household had a refrigerator nor access to ice. Ice was even shipped all over the world so people could use it to chill their food and make it last.

Chapter One: Importance of Food Preservation and Storage

Today, chilling (or refrigeration) and freezing are the most basic food storage techniques. To keep food fresh and safe to eat, one just needs to store it at a low temperature. This method is so simple and necessitates very minimal to zero preparation.

The cold from a refrigerator or freezer delays the growth of bacteria and other microorganisms, preserves food quality and reduces spoilage. If stored properly, some food items can last for a few days inside a refrigerator or freezer while others can stay fresh for weeks or even months. Bacteria cannot grow on frozen food so when you freeze food, they stay safe for long periods of time. For instance, you can store red meat in the freezer for as long as four to twelve months but only up to five days if you keep it in the refrigerator. You can keep leftover cooked meat for two to six months when you store it in the freezer and it will only last for three days when it is just in the refrigerator. However, even if it won't spoil for a long time, the taste and texture will deteriorate over time, depending on the kind of food that is stored so it is best to use frozen food within a few months.

Chapter One: Importance of Food Preservation and Storage

Here are some safety reminders concerning refrigerating and freezing food:

- Your refrigerator should have a temperature that ranges from 1°C and 4°C. If you are storing food for commercial purposes, you are required by law to use temperatures below 8°C.

- Make sure you label your foods with "use by" or "best before" dates if you will take them away from their original packages.

- Observe the First In First Out system when it comes to storing food. This means that you use foods that have the nearest "use by" or "best before" dates.

- Make sure you observe proper stock rotation.

- There should be plenty of room in your freezer or refrigerator. This will ensure proper circulation. If you overload your units, the food will not be stored properly.

Chapter One: Importance of Food Preservation and Storage

- To avoid cross contamination, it is good to utilize separate refrigerators for ready-to-eat foods and raw ones that are usually high risk. If you cannot have separate refrigerators, you should use separate shelves on the fridge. The best practice is to place the ready-to-eat foods on top of raw foods.

- When you have food from a can, make sure that you put it in a separate container. Do not refrigerate an open can.

- The freezer temperature should range from -18°C and -22°C.

- Food that will be kept in freezers should be in properly wrapped in freezer bags or air-tight containers. Meat that has freezer burn can be unfit for consumption.

- You should freeze food items before their "use by" or "best before" dates.

Chapter One: Importance of Food Preservation and Storage

- Once you have defrosted food, you should not put them back in the freezer. Thawing allows microorganisms an opportunity to develop. Once you have thawed food, use it immediately. If you are not able to use it, you can chill it in the refrigerator for no more than 24 hours.

- To keep your freezer a safe place for storage, make sure to defrost it regularly.

- Meat and poultry should be kept in their package until it is time for use. If you are planning to store meat and poultry for longer than two months, then you should overwrap the original packages with freezer paper, heavy-duty plastic wrap or airtight foil.

- In case of power outage, do not open your freezer door. The frozen food will stay frozen for about 24 hours so you can still have frozen food until power returns.

Chapter One: Importance of Food Preservation and Storage

According to the FDA, not all product "use by" or "best before" dates are a safe guide. It is important to observe the shot yet safe time limits on refrigerating and freezing foods so that you can prevent them from spoiling or becoming unsafe to eat. You should remember to observe the handling recommendations indicated on your food product.

Here is a chart that you can refer to when it comes to length of food storage in refrigerators and freezers for good food quality:

Food Product	In Refrigerator	In Freezer
Eggs (in shell)	3 to 5 weeks	Do not freeze
Raw Egg Yolks and Egg Whites	2 to 4 days	1 year
Hard Cooked Eggs	1 week	Do not Freeze
TV Dinners		3 to 4 months
Vegetable Soup	3 to 4 days	2 to 3 months
Soup with Meat	3 to 4 days	2 to 3 months
Store-prepared Deli	3 to 5 days	Do not Freeze
Pre-stuffed meat	1 day	Do not Freeze

Chapter One: Importance of Food Preservation and Storage

Commercial Vacuum-Packed Dinners	3 to 4 days	Do not Freeze
Bacon	7 days	1 month
Smoked Patties	7 days	1 to 2 months
Raw Sausage	1 to 2 days	1 to 2 months
Fresh Steaks	3 to 5 days	6 to 12 months
Fresh Chops	3 to 5 days	4 to 6 months
Roasts	3 to 5 days	4 to 12 months
Variety Meats	1 to 2 days	3 to 4 months
Leftover Cooked Meat	3 to 4 days	2 to 3 months
Leftover meat broth / gravy	1 to 2 days	2 to 3 months
Fresh Poultry – whole	1 to 2 days	1 year
Fresh Poultry – parts	1 to 2 days	9 months
Fresh Giblets	1 to 2 days	3 to 4 months
Leftover Cooked Poultry – Fried	3 to 4 days	4 months

Chapter One: Importance of Food Preservation and Storage

Chicken		
Leftover cooked poultry dishes	3 to 4 days	4 to 6 months
Chicken Nuggets	3 to 4 days	1 to 3 months
Raw Hamburger	1 to 2 days	3 to 4 months
Raw Ground turkey, lamb or pork	1 to 2 days	3 to 4 months
Corned beef in pouch	5 to 7 days	1 month (need to be drained)
Fresh seafood	1 – 2 days	3 to 6 months
Canned seafood (out of can)	3 to 4 days	2 months
Lean Fish	1 to 2 days	6 to 8 months
Fatty Fish	1 to 2 days	2 to 3 months
Cooked Fish	3 to 4 days	4 to 6 months
Smoked Fish	14 days	2 months

Chapter One: Importance of Food Preservation and Storage

Chapter Two: Other Methods of Food Preservation

Throughout history, food preservation has been a wonderful way of making sure -that food gets to the table safe and can be stored for future use. Every culture has its own way to harness nature and preserve food in order to ensure survival. From ancient methods of sun-drying and salting to modern food dehydration and canning, the journey of food preservation has been long and rich, and yet there is no end to the innovations! There are always fresh discoveries and new methods to preserve, store and consume food.

Chapter Two: Other Methods of Food Preservation

Salting

Salt is used to preserve food because when it is applied it draws out water molecules from the food, replacing them with salt molecules. The process is called osmosis. In essence, the salting stops when the amount of salt is the same inside and outside of the food. Salting stops the growth of bacteria and other microorganisms. It may even destroy bacteria when used in high concentrations. However, too much salt can make food unappetizing.

History will show the value of salt in preserving food. Many people have dried meat, fish and vegetable produce over the years. Salt is such a highly precious commodity that it was used by Ancient Romans as a form of currency. There are two ways of salting, dry and wet curing:

Dry Curing

Dry Curing is a method of applying salt directly to the food and leaving it for a time so that the salt can draw the water content out. This is usually used for meat products.

Chapter Two: Other Methods of Food Preservation

Wet Curing

Wet Curing or Brine is a method wherein salt is mixed with water before being added to the food. This method is also often used with canning.

Salting is a simple way to pickle, ferment and store vegetables such as leafy greens including kale, spinach, bok choy and chard, celery, cabbage, runner beans, cauliflower florets, shelled peas and green beans. These vegetables are usually blanched first before they are dry salted. Corn is another product that can be dry salted.

Use of excessive salt is harmful to health. When you salt to preserve your food, you should always follow salting recipes as indicated. It is also advisable to only use salt that is particularly designed for the purpose such as Kosher salt and pickling salt.

Sugaring

Sugaring is another food preservation method that reduced the water content of the food item. When you store

Chapter Two: Other Methods of Food Preservation

food items in a high-sugar environment, you stop the growth of bacteria and other microorganisms. Think of jelly, jam and marmalade. You can make fruits and vegetables last a long time then can them for proper storage. You will learn more about canning in another part of this book.

You can use sugar granules, honey, or sugar syrup to preserve food. All kinds of sugary substances will work. Popular vegetables that are sugared include carrots and ginger as they are used for condiments or relishes. Apples, plums, cherries apricots, and peaches are some of the fruits that can be preserved by sugaring. You can also use sugar and mix it with salt to preserve certain meats and fishes. Others mix sugar with another liquid and make a brine to preserve meats.

While using excessive sugar may be a risk to health, using less can mean that food may spoil. If you are going to preserve food by sugaring, you should follow the recipe and use the right amount so that you will be able to preserve the food properly and safely. It is also important to remember that sugared foods should be taken in moderation. An average person can take in six times the recommended amount of sugar if not moderated.

Vacuum Packing

One of the purposes of vacuum packing is to extend the storage life of a product. Vacuum packing is a packaging technique in which air is removed from inside before a package is sealed. Vacuum packing can be done manually or automatically. This method is similar to canning, the food preservation method that will be discussed at length throughout this book. Food that is vacuum packed does not last as long as canned goods.

Vacuum packing creates an airtight atmosphere, eliminating oxygen that can give bacteria an opportunity to develop in food. The best thing about vacuum packing is that you can preserve the quality of the food without adding extra ingredients such as sugar, salt and other elements as with canning. If you want to cook meat rare, then vacuum packing is your best option for storage because it can preserve the taste, smell, color and texture of the food as it

Chapter Two: Other Methods of Food Preservation

retains moisture. Even chefs use vacuum packing in food preparation so that their specific ingredients will produce exceptional results when cooked. As they say, with vacuum packing, you get air out and lock freshness in.

Here are some guidelines on how to vacuum pack food in safe manner:

- Food should be prepared hygienically. Always wash vegetables and fruits. Take out unwanted fat, bone and skin from meat before packing.

- The food should be stored in a suitable vacuum packing bag.

- Use a vacuum packing machine according to instructions.

- Keep the vacuum packed food in a cool, dry place (shelf) or in the refrigerator.

- There are certain packing methods that won't require the use of a machine, but you may have different

Chapter Two: Other Methods of Food Preservation

results and you won't be entirely sure about the safety and quality of the food.

- You can vacuum pack many different kinds of foods such as Meat, fish, poultry, soups and sauces, fruits, vegetables, flour, cereal, nuts, coffee and even homemade cookies! It is important to remember that vegetables should be correctly blanched before they are kept in vacuum packs and frozen.

- Blanching will remove dirt and bacteria as well as stop the enzyme action that spoils your vegetables' color, texture and flavor. You should avoid vacuum packing cabbage, broccoli, mushrooms and Brussels sprouts as these veggies produce gases that can expand your packaging and cause spoilage. The same is true for cheese.

- It is essential that vegetables are correctly blanched before freezing, as blanching removes dirt and bacteria. Most importantly, blanching stops the enzyme action which destroys the fresh flavor, color, and texture of your vegetables. Watch your vegetables carefully as you blanch. Under-blanching actually stimulates enzyme action and over-blanching removes color and vitamins.

You can vacuum seal a lot of foods, but you should avoid soft cheese, mushrooms, broccoli, cabbage, and Brussels sprouts. They give off gases that expand the bag and lead to spoilage.

Canning

If done correctly, you can extend the lifespan of your food through canning. Similar to vacuum packing, you remove the oxygen from food using an airtight seal and store it in a sugary, salty or acidic environment that deprives bacteria of the opportunity to grow. In the succeeding chapters, this book will discuss in length the process of canning, how to do it safely even at home and its advantages.

Chapter Two: Other Methods of Food Preservation

Here is a brief overview: canning is more complex that just putting something in an airtight container. It is often referred to as sterilization because heat is used to eliminate any microorganism that can cause food to spoil as well as lethal toxins that are dangerous to people. It Canning is based on the principle that for every 10° C increase in the temperature used in treating food, bacteria is destroyed tenfold. Moreover, when food is exposed to high temperatures at short periods of time, without reaching boiling point, it retains its natural flavor even as it is stored in containers.

Food is placed in jars or like containers and then heated—during the heating, air is removed out of the containers and as it cools down, a vacuum seal is produced, meaning air which can bring contaminating bacteria and microorganisms cannot enter.

Canning food is very beneficial for people who have their own farms or gardens as they can preserve the food they have grown for storage throughout droughts, winter or

Chapter Two: Other Methods of Food Preservation

even for emergencies. Depending on the kind of food that is canned, it can be stored from years to decades!

Here are some of the types of foods that can be canned:

Fruit. You can store fruit through canning with the boiling water bath method. Fruits have a high acid content, usually 4.0 pH, which prevents the growth of Clostridium botulinum spores. Fruits such as pears, nectarines, apples, peaches, plums, blackberries, raspberries, blueberries, strawberries and seckels are great for canning. You can make them into jams, jellies, pickles and fruit preserves.

Pickled Condiments. With the boiling bath water method, you can also can relishes, sauces, pickles, chutneys and vinegars.

Vegetables, Seafood, Meat and Poultry. These are foods that contain low acid and they are not easy to preserve via canning. You need to use a pressure canner to ensure that the output will be free of Clostridium botulinum spores that can cause botulism.

Chapter Two: Other Methods of Food Preservation

There are two methods of canning: water bath and pressure canning. If you are canning fruits and other foods that have high acid content, you should use the water bath canning method. This is a faster way of canning which will keep the food safe to eat for a minimum of one year. Pressure canning is utilized for non-acidic food such as meat, complete meals, poultry, seafood and vegetables. Unlike fruits vegetables, especially corn, beets, green beans, and vegetable mixtures are usually non-acidic. You will need a pressure canning equipment for this method. You will also have to use a pressure canner when you are storing low-acidic foods mixed with high-acidic ones.

A pressure canner is a pot that has a pressure gauge. Between the container and its lid is a unique locking mechanism located between the lid and the container. A vent pipe located atop the pressure canner's lid allows steam to seep out. There are many factors that will ensure food safety when it comes to canning such as altitude, contents, temperature, etc. These items should be taken into consideration and recipes/instructions should be followed carefully to ensure safe preservation.

Chapter Two: Other Methods of Food Preservation

Food preservation is such an exciting, beneficial, strategic, and often profitable, venture. Different kinds of methods help delay, reduce or prevent spoilage of food, extend shelf life, create nutritional value, and maintain flavor, texture and other food quality.

Now that you have an idea of different kinds of food preservation methods, dive in to the wonderful world of canning!

Chapter Three: All About Canning

You may be familiar with canned tomatoes, canned sardines, canned mushroom soup… and many other canned foods. When you go to the supermarket, you will see lines upon lines of spam, canned baked beans, asparagus, fish, ham, tuna, peaches pears, tomato soup, pineapples, pineapple juice, tomato juice, Vienna sausage and different veggies. These are just examples of food products that are preserved and stored using the canning method.

Canning is a food preservation technique in which a variety of food is processed and sealed in airtight containers so that their shelf life can last from one up to five years.

Chapter Three: All About Canning

Even though you are not in a commercial food business, it is good to know about canning, especially if you have your own garden or you grow your own food. Wouldn't it be nice to be able to enjoy your produce even though they are not in season, and to be able to store your bounty so that they don't have to go to waste? Canning will not only give you the opportunity to stock up on food supplies, but also ensure that you will never lack for nutritious food options.

Before you delve into the whole process of canning, here is a list of food choices that can be preserved through the method. You can even use this list to plan what you can plant next in your garden, as there are both excellent and food choices for vegetables and fruits that can be preserved.

First of all, you need to know that throughout the course of this book, the term canning does not always refer to the use of metal cans as with commercial canning. When it comes to home canning, people store food in glass jars. Since bottling or jarring can have a negative connotation, the term canning has been a widely accepted term for storing food in jars and creating a vacuum seal in order to preserve them.

Before You Start Canning

Now that you know that there are many, if not almost all, kinds of foods can be preserved through canning, you need to understand the basics of the technique. Canning or bottling (for home canning) involves strict methods because if proper procedures are not observed, people can get sick or even die from food that they have canned. Quite important is keeping your workplace hygienic and pristine. Everything that you use for canning should be sterile throughout the whole process. When this is observed, it is unlikely for food poisoning issues to occur.

Understanding that different foods have different acidity levels will also help you determine what kind of canning method to use. Foods are categorized into two groups: high-acid and low-acid. You need to use the appropriate procedure so that you can ensure the prevention

Chapter Three: All About Canning

of bacterial growth. Before canning something, make sure to determine the acidity level of that fruit, vegetable or meat.

High Acid Foods + Boiling Water Canner

Foods that have an acidity level of no more than 4.6 pH need to be canned using boiling water method. At sea level, this procedure will heat the food to 212°F (boiling point) and kill bacteria, molds and yeast that may be present in the food. The natural acid in the food, often fruits, will keep the bacteria that bring about botulism from growing.

Low Acid Foods + Pressure Canner

Foods that have an acidity level of greater than 4.6 pH require the use of a pressure canner. Low acid foods may need an acid substance, like vinegar or lemon juice, so that they will be safe for canning. The pressure canner can raise temperatures that will destroy botulism bacteria in these types of food. When mixing low acid and high acid foods, the mixture is considered as low acid.

Chapter Three: All About Canning

Clostridium botulinum bacteria can thrive in a sealed jar of food, if the wrong method is used. This bacteria can create a poisonous toxin that can be fatal when ingested (botulism). Even simply tasting food that contains this poison can cause people to die. When you are boiling food at altitudes below 1,000 feet, it should be done for 10 minutes to destroy these bacteria. When boiling at altitudes over 1,000 feet, food should be boiled for an additional 1 minute per 1,000 feet of extra elevation. Boiling would mean that big, foamy bubbles are formed and breaking out over the liquid on the surface the food. To prevent the risk of botulism, make sure that you use the appropriate method of canning for the food selection

Tools and Equipment

There may be canning tools that are already available in your home. There will be other tools and equipment that you may need to purchase.

- Large stockpots
- Glass storage jars
- Jar lids (metal)
- Metal rings

Chapter Three: All About Canning

- Stainless steel tongs
- Lid lifter
- Jar lifter

The large stockpots will be used for the boiling water bath method and when you sterilize your jars. You can reuse your jar cans and rings. The jar lids, however, will have to be new every time you can.

You may have to purchase a pressure canner if you will produce in large batches and if you will do it regularly. While it may cost a lot, it will be a good investment. When you can low-acid foods, you can do it safely using a pressure canner.

Best Vegetables for Canning

To get an idea of which vegetables are suitable for canning, take stock of the canned vegetables that can be found in your local grocery store. Commercially canned vegetable products can be readily duplicated at home. Packing veggies in glass jars and sealing the product with airtight lids will ensure that there will be no bacterial growth and you can prolong the life of your veggies for future enjoyment.

- Tomatoes
- Asparagus
- Potatoes
- Carrots
- Peas
- Beans
- Cabbage
- Peppers
- Winter squash
- Beets
- Corn

Tomatoes, which are usually found in many home gardens in abundance, can be preserved as paste and as blanched whole tomatoes. You can also create a pasta sauce and seal it in jars. Most vegetables need to be blanched before canning while others can be packed raw and drenched with boiling water before sealing.

Chapter Three: All About Canning

Best Fruits for Canning

Canned fruits are a pantry staple. The following fruits become superior in quality when they are canned compared to when they are simply frozen:

- Pears
- Plums
- Peaches
- Apricots
- Grapes
- Pineapple
- Nectarine

You can use water, fruit juice or fruit syrup when canning fruits. Usually, syrups help hold the shape, flavor and color of the fruit being canned. Fruit can be canned safely by raw packing or by hot packing. Raw packing means you need to wash slice and pack the fruit without the need to pre-heat it. This is a faster method of canning and requires less work. You will have buoyant fruit pieces that usually float to the surface of the liquid that you used for canning. This output of this method is often referred to as fruit floats. The issue with fruit floats is that the top layers of your fruits are sticking above the liquid and will eventually turn brown. While the fruit will not spoil, it certainly does not look appetizing with such color. When you use the hot pack method, you can produce higher quality of canned fruit.

Canning Meat and Poultry

As long as you use good quality products, you should be able to can red meat, poultry, fish, game and other seafood. The general tips you need to follow include:

- Before canning, you need to chill home-produced meat to lower than 40°F, soon after the animal is slaughtered in order to avoid spoilage.
- Meat should be frozen if it will be kept longer before canning. Frozen meat should be stored at 0°F.
- Meat should be trimmed of bruised spots, fat and gristle before it is processed for canning. Fatty meat can cause failures in sealing.

Chapter Three: All About Canning

Different kinds of meat that can be canned are: chicken, goose, duck turkey, game birds, beef, pork, lamb, sausage, venison, veal, rabbit, and fish. Meat can be canned in strips, chunks or cubes. Meat broth can also be canned. Meat mixtures such as chili con carne are also suitable for canning.

Pressure canning is the only method that is acceptable for canning vegetables, meat, poultry, and seafood. These low-acid foods that can be home to Clostridium botulinum (the bacteria that causes botulism) should be processed in pressure canners with the correct amount of pressure, temperature and duration. When done properly, the bacteria are killed. Boiling water technique will not work and will only pose the risk of food poisoning.

Hot Packed vs. Raw Packed Foods

Now that you have your food selection, your jars and equipment, you are ready to can. You can choose from two different canning procedures: hot packing and raw packing.

Chapter Three: All About Canning

Hot packing is the method of cooking freshly prepared food using heat to boiling point, then allowing it to simmer for about 2 to 5 minutes. The boiled food will be put in jars. Raw packing, on the other hand, is the method of filling jars with freshly prepared food, but without heating them. Raw packing is more suitable to processing vegetables with the use of pressure canners. Usually raw packed fruit will float in jars and air that is trapped may cause food to discolor after 2 to 3 months of storage.

Regardless of the method, the water, syrup or juice that is added to the foods should be heated to boiling point before pouring them into the jars. Doing so would allow the removal of air from the food tissues and keeps the food from floating to the top. Removing air would also shrink the food and increase the vacuum inside, improving the shelf life of the processed food. If you will use a boiling water canner, then hot-packing is the best method to pack your food. Hot packing also allows you to produce more superior quality of food in terms of color and flavor.

Chapter Three: All About Canning

Practicing Safe Home Canning

Canning involves many steps and if you are new to it, it is best to read thoroughly and learn all that you can before you jump into the process. You should always follow time-tested and current practices for home canning to ensure the success of your endeavor. You want to be able to preserve and food safely and not cause any harm to yourself or your loved ones. Here are practical safe home canning tips you need to remember and observe:

Hygiene

- Always wash your hands with soap and water before you do anything in the kitchen.

- Wash fruits, vegetables and kitchen utensils and make sure that surfaces are clean to eliminate the risk of bacterial growth and food-related sicknesses.

- Fruits should be washed under cool, running water.

Chapter Three: All About Canning

- One cutting board should be used for produce. Another should be used for raw meat, fish, poultry and seafood. Never use the same cutting board for all kinds of food.

- Always have paper towels handy so that you can wipe kitchen surfaces as necessary.

- Use dishcloths and change them regularly to prevent cross-contamination. Do not use sponges.

- Make sure that countertops are sanitized, as well as utensils and cutting boards before and after you use them for preparing food.

- Make sure to clean before, during and after the canning process.

Chapter Three: All About Canning

Cooking

Canning involves use of high temperatures and this method kills bacteria. Home canning will require your full attention to avoid botulism. You can protect yourself and your family by observing the following:

- Know when to use a boiling water and a pressure canner depending on the food acidity

- Make sure to add acid to low acid foods.

- Do not change the pressure level or the duration of processing. When you substitute, you can affect the time and pressure and allow the botulism bacteria to stay in the finished product.

- Make sure that the heating temperature as well as the steam pressure is maintained by checking it from time to time.

- Each batch has a process, so remember it.

Chapter Three: All About Canning

- Use safe and proper tools and equipment. There are specific jars for home canning.

- Use self-sealing lids.

- Old lids should be thrown away and not reused, even if they are still in good condition.

- Do not substitute the jar size or the quantity of ingredients.

- Make sure you leave the recommended space at the top of the jar—not too little and not too much as this can affect the process.

- Use only tested home canning recipes.

Storing Canned Products

- Make sure to label your home-canned foods prior to storage

- Home canned goods should be kept in a cool, dry place.

- When a home-canned product is opened, the left over should be refrigerated. If it is a home-canned seafood, it should be refrigerated immediately and leftovers are thrown out three days after opening

- All canned foods should be used within one year so you can enjoy the best quality.

A lot of home canned products are immensely popular as gifts. If you are planning to preserve your food or give them as gifts, make sure that you follow food safety conditions when it comes to canning or bottling.

How Canning Preserves Foods

A lot of foods have high water content—this is the reason they perish or spoil easily. Water becomes an agent for undesirable microorganisms such as yeast mold and bacteria to thrive on. These microorganisms also multiply

Chapter Three: All About Canning

inside diseased, damaged or bruised food. Food spoils because of enzyme activity and oxygen reactions. Enzymes and oxygen are active non fresh food tissues. Similarly, food can lose its quality when there is moisture loss. Canning or bottling helps stop food spoilage and preserves the quality of food so it can be enjoyed at a later time.

Proper canning involves various procedures including washing and peeing fresh food, hot packing, adding acids, using jars and self-sealing lids, and processing said jars or bottles in pressure canner or boiling water for an appropriate period of time. The collective processes do the following:

- Remove oxygen
- Eliminate enzymes
- Deter the growth of yeast, mold and bacteria
- Form a high vacuum

Chapter Three: All About Canning

Canning keeps the liquid in and the air out. That means the food remains fresh without the risk of microorganism contamination. While all canning processes vary, there are three basic steps:

Processing

This is the stage in which food is selected, washed, peeled, sliced, cubed, chopped, shelled, pitted, boned, cooked or added with acid.

Sealing

Once the food is processed, it is sealed in cans or bottles.

Heating

The sealed cans are then heated to certain temperatures at set periods of time so that the harmful bacteria are killed and spoilage is prevented.

After these stages, the canned food is ready for shelf storage and becomes safe to consume for a period of at least on year to 5 years, sometimes even longer.

Chapter Three: All About Canning

Does Canning Affect Nutritional Levels of Food?

People normally believe that canned foods contain fewer nutrients than fresh or frozen ones.

Canned foods are often thought to be less nutritious than fresh or frozen foods, but research shows that this is not always true. Canning can preserve a lot of nutrients contained in food. For instance, carbs, protein and fat remain unaffected by the processes involved in canning. Vitamins A, D, K and E are fat soluble and easily preserved along with most minerals. Studies have shown that some foods that are rich in nutrients maintain the same level of nutrients after they are canned. However, vitamin B and Vitamin C can be damaged in the process as they are water soluble and sensitive to heat.

Canning can also boost the amounts of other healthy compounds found in food such as antioxidants. For instance, corn and tomatoes will produce more antioxidants when they are heated, so canned corn and canned tomatoes are better sources of antioxidants than fresh ones.

Chapter Three: All About Canning

Some nutrient levels decrease and some nutrient levels increase because of the canning process. This just means that some canned foods are comparable or as good as fresh or frozen foods.

Chapter Four: Canning Techniques

This chapter discusses general information on canning elements and procedures. If you have never tried home canning before and you want to do it now, make sure that you understand the basics. Here are guidelines and helpful data from the National Home Center for Food Preparation about canning safely.

Chapter Four: Canning Techniques

Jars and Lids

- Only mason-jar type canning jars should be used. These sizes of these jars are large enough for the size specified in most canning recipes of most foods.

- Make sure to purchase only the number of lids that you will be able to use in a year and not more. The lids you use should always be new. Additionally, you should follow the manufacturer's instructions for lid preparation.

- Use lids that are two-piece and self-sealing.

- Avoid mayonnaise-type jars especially for foods that will be pressure canned. The jars may break.

- When it comes to filing jars, you should remove air bubbles by using a plastic spatula or knife. Never use a metal one. Insert the spatula or knife between the food and the inside surface in your jar then move it up and down, slowly turning your jar, so that bubbles can escape.

- Always clean the rim of the jar which is the sealing surface using a damp paper towel or clean cloth. Adjust the headspace according to the instructions and do not overfill the jar.

- After cleaning, place the lid with the gasket facing down and fit the metal band screw upon the flat lid. Always follow the manufacturer's guidelines concerning tightening jar lids.

Boiling Water Canning

Boiling water canning is used for high-acid foods. The boiling water canners are made of either porcelain–covered steel or aluminum. There is one variety of boiling water canner that is made of stainless steel.

Chapter Four: Canning Techniques

Boiling water canners should have removable racks and fitted lids. The racks can be shaped wires or perforated ones. The boiling water canner should have a depth that can allow for at least one inch of briskly boiling water over the jar tops when then are processing. If you have a smooth top range, you should get a canner that has a flat bottom. Some canners are not entirely flat and cannot be used on electric burners. If you are using a gas burner, you can get a ridged bottom or a flat boiling water canner.

The boiling water canner should not be wider than 4 inches in diameter so that there will be even heating when you process jars. Your boing water canner should not be more than two inches beyond your burner range.

Make sure you get the right boiling water caner for a successful canning. Following are the steps you need to follow; make sure that you read them thoroughly and read through completely before you begin the process.

Chapter Four: Canning Techniques

1. Before food preparation, put your canner rack in the bottom of your boiling water canner and fill the canner with clean water up to half, if you are going to load it with pint jars.

2. If you are different sizes or quantity of jars, the water level should be adjusted—it should be 1 to 2 inches covering the top of the jars.

3. Put the boiling water canner over the center of your burner and preheat the water to about 180°F for hot packed foods and only 140°F for raw-packed foods.

4. While you are preheating the boiling water canner, you can prepare the food for the jars.

5. After preparing the food, put them in the jars accordingly, depending on the method you use, whether hot packing or raw packing. Seal the jars and fit them with ring bands and lids.

Chapter Four: Canning Techniques

6. Load the filled and sealed jars into the canner, one by one, with the use of a jar lifter. Place the jar lifter securely under the neck of the jar so that you can move them upright. If you tilt the jar, spillage may enter the sealing area.

7. You can also utilize a shaped wire rack that can hold your jars in a raised position inside the canner. Make sure to use the handles as you lower the rack into the water so there won't be any tilting.

8. The water level should be at least one inch above the jar covers so you can add more boiling water as necessary. Remember to pour boiling water around the jars and not on top of them. If the food you are processing will require 30 minutes, then you should have a 2-inch water level above your jars.

9. The heating should be in the highest level and the canner is covered so that the water will boil vigorously.

Chapter Four: Canning Techniques

10. You should have a timer so you can accurately monitor the time required to process the food.

11. The boiling water caner should be covered for the whole duration of the processing. The boiling should be maintained even if you adjust the heat setting.

12. Should the boiling stop, you need to adjust the heat to the highest setting so that the water will boil vigorously again. The timing will start over.

13. After the jars have been boiled for the required time, you can turn the heat off and open the lid. Do not move the jars yet. Wait for five minutes before taking them oyt so that the contents can settle.

14. Use a jar lifter when taking out the jars. Again, the jars should not tilt.

Chapter Four: Canning Techniques

15. Place the jars on a cooling rack or a towel with at least one inch space in between. Allow them to cool down. Do not place the jars directly on a cold surface.

16. The jars should remain undisturbed for about 12 to 24 hours.

17. You should not push the center of the lids down nor tighten the ring bands until the jar is absolutely cooled.

18. Once completely cooled, you can remove the ring bands from the jars that are sealed.

19. If you processed unsealed jars, make sure that they are used or consumed first.

20. You can wash your jars and lids to remove all sorts of residue. You can re-use jars but you cannot re-use lids for future canning.

Chapter Four: Canning Techniques

- You should label your jars so that you remember when they were processed and until when they are safe to eat or use.

- Store the jars in a dry and cool place that is not in direct light.

Pressure Canning

Previously, pressure canners were mostly used in commercial canning. But they have been extensively redesigned for home use during the 1970s as more and more people preserved food using the canning technique. Pressure canners are fitted with an automatic vent pipe, an automatic vent lock, removable racks, a dial gauge, and a safety fuse. Modern pressure canners usually come as thin-walled kettles and are very lightweight unlike their traditional counterparts that were heavy-walled and had turn-on lids. Make sure to purchase and use pressure canners that have the Underwriter's Laboratory seal for safety purposes.

Chapter Four: Canning Techniques

For a successful pressure canning, make sure to do the following steps:

1. Before you even start preparing your food, check to ensure that the pressure canning is working properly. The gaskets, gauge, lid and other parts should be in order, the vent pipes should be clean and there should be no mineral deposits or other trapped materials in it.

2. Place the pressure canner in the center of your burner, making sure that the range and burner are level. If the burner produces too much heat, it can seriously damage your pressure canner. Usually, an outdoor gas burner is not used for pressure canners.

3. Place the hot water and the rack inside your pressure canner. There should be a specified amount of water in the instructions or recipe. But if there is none, you should have about two to three inches of water in the container. If the food requires a longer process, you will have to use more water. Make sure you abide by

Chapter Four: Canning Techniques

USDA guidelines on pressure canning specific foods so you know the amount of water you need to use.

4. Preheat the water to about 180°F for hot packed foods. But you should not boil it too long that the water will decrease. Heat to 140 °F for raw-packed foods.

5. Once you finished preparing the foods and filled the jars, fir the lids and ring bands and seal the jars. Use a jar lifter to put the filled jars into jar rack of the pressure canner. Make sure that the jars are always upright throughout the movement as tilting may cause spillage.

6. The canner's lid should be securely fastened. You can open the petcock or take the weight off the vent pipe.

7. The heat setting should be in the highest level. The water should be heated until it boils and steam is flowing freely from the petcock or open vent. You will notice it as a funnel-shape steam. Maintain the high

heat setting for 10 continuous minutes as you let the steam flow out.

8. When the exhausting (letting steam out) is done, close the pet cock or put the counterweight back on the vent pipe. Allow the pressure canner to pressurize for the next three to ten minutes.

9. You should start timing the procedure as soon as you dial gauge reading reaches the recommended pressure. If your pressure canner does not come with a dial gauge, you will notice the weighted gauge will begin to juggle when the recommended pressure has been reached—start timing then.

10. The heat should be regulated so that you can maintain a steady pressure. When there is loss of pressure, there will be under - processing and the final product will be unsafe food. Pressure variations can also cause liquids losses.

Chapter Four: Canning Techniques

11. If the pressure is lost and it goes below the recommendation, you should bring your pressure canner back to the required pressure and reset the timing of the process with the original required process time as indicated.

12. Once the process time is completed, turn the heat off. Take the pressure canner out of the electric burner and let it naturally cool down. Never slide the canner. You should lift it when you move it. You can also leave it on the burner once you turn it off if you know that you cannot move the canner without tilting or tipping it over, or if the canner is too heavy.

13. As the pressure canner is cooling down, it is de-pressuring. You should ever force fool the canner by pouring cool water over it or opening the vent pipe immediately. If you force-cool a canner, you may risk food spoilage. There may also be seal failures, loss of liquid and warped lids as a result of forced cooling.

Chapter Four: Canning Techniques

14. Take extra caution when removing the weight from the vent pipe. Even if the dial gauge has cooled down, do not attempt to open the canner unless the dial indicates zero pounds pressure. You can tilt the weight a little so that no steam will escape as you pull the vent pipe away. If the cover locks are not released, do not force the lids to open.

15. If you are using an old pressure canner model, they don't come with dial gauges and you would have to time depressurization. If it is a standard-sized, heavy-walled pressure canner, you will have to time 30 minutes of depressurization when it is loaded with pint jars. If it is loaded with quart jars, then the depressurization is 45 minutes. If it is a new, thin-walled pressure canner, the vent locks will automatically open when the pressure is out. The piston of the vent lock will drop and release the lock. Do not force open this lock.

Chapter Four: Canning Techniques

16. Once the pressure canner is depressurized, you have to open the petcock or take out the weight of the vent pipe. After 10 minutes of waiting time, you can unfasten the lid and cautiously remove it. Make sure that you pull up the lid with the underside facing away from you so that the steam will not burn you.

17. Use a jar lifter to remove the jars one by one. Do not tilt the jars.

18. Place them on a cooling rack or a towel, with at least a one inch space in between jars. Do not place them directly on cold surfaces.

19. The jars should be left undisturbed for 12 to 24 hours s they can cool down.

20. You should not push the center of the lids down nor tighten the ring bands until the jar is absolutely cooled.

Chapter Four: Canning Techniques

21. Once completely cooled, you can remove the ring bands from the jars that are sealed.

22. You can wash your jars and lids to remove all sorts of residue. You can re-use jars but you cannot re-use lids for future canning.

23. You should label your jars so that you remember when they were processed and until when they are safe to eat or use.

24. Store the jars in a dry and cool place that is not in direct light.

25. Don't forget to dry your pressure canner, gasket and lid. All removable parts such as the safety valves and petcocks should be taken out, washed and dried very well. Observe the manufacturer's maintenance and storage guidelines.

Chapter Four: Canning Techniques

Canned Foods for Special Diets

If you have a special diet or you have a family member or friend that requires one, then you know that special diet foods which are commercially canned are quite costly. You can choose to can at home to produce low-salt and low-sugar foods. Even if the flavor, texture and color of the food may not be as appealing as commercially canned foods, you can be sure that you are getting healthy, less expensive foods for special diet needs.

Canning without Sugar

You can fruits without adding sugar, especially if you are preparing it for a special diet.

- Choose fully ripe fruits that are firm.
- Never use overripe fruits.
- Use the hot pack method.
- Use water instead of sugar syrup.

- You can also use unsweetened fruit juice, especially if it comes from the fruit that you are canning.
- Sugar substitutes can be added when serving.

Canning with less or without Salt

You can vegetable by adding little to no salt, especially if you are preparing it for a special diet. The only issue is that the little amount of salt can season the food but it may not ensure food safety. Salt substitutes can be added when serving, as needed.

Maintaining Color and Flavor in Canned Food

In order to keep a good natural color and to maintain quality flavor with your stored canned food, be sure to:

- Remove all oxygen from your jar and from the food tissues.
- Destroy food enzymes quickly.
- Use high quality jar vacuums and airtight seals.

Chapter Four: Canning Techniques

To achieve the above, you must observe these guidelines during canning processing and storage:

1. Make sure you use high-quality foods to process.

2. It is best to use the hot pack method when you are canning acidic foods.

3. As much as you can, do not expose the food to air.

4. Can food harvested or slaughtered as early as possible.

5. If you are preparing many jars of food, keep fruits such as apples, pears, apricots, peaches, and nectarines that are already sliced, halved, quartered or diced in a solution water solution that has ascorbic acid. Combine 3 grams of ascorbic acid with 1 gallon of cold water. This way you can maintain freshness and avoid discoloration can also use the same solution for potatoes, grapes, cherries and

Chapter Four: Canning Techniques

mushrooms. Ascorbic acid is available in different forms: tablets, powder and commercial mixes. If you will use powdered vitamin C, one level teaspoon is about 3 grams and you can add that to a gallon of water for the treatment solution. For vitamin C tablets, get six 500-mg tablets, crush it and dissolve them in a gallon of water to prepare the solution. You can also purchase seasonally available commercial mixes of citric and ascorbic acid from supermarkets. Make sure to follow manufacturer's instructions t make the treatment solution.

6. Make sure that you observe the right headspace when you are filling the jars with hot food.

7. Securely tighten—but not too strongly—the screw bands.

8. Always cool jars down after processing, without moving them.

9. Store them in areas with temperatures between 50 to 70 degrees Fahrenheit.

10. It is advisable to only can food that you can use / consume within a year, unless you are producing them commercially.

Equipment and Methods that are Not Recommended

When canning food and processing filled jars, the use of open-kettles, microwave ovens, conventional ovens and dishwashers are not recommended for the reason of using the said equipment does not ensure the prevention of spoilage. Steam canners are also not recommended until further research is completed.

The use of canning powders that are very popular as preservatives is also not recommended as heat processing is essential to canning.

Chapter Four: Canning Techniques

The following containers are also not recommended for canning:

- o Jars with glass caps
- o Jars with wire bails
- o Zinc caps
- o Zinc porcelain-lined caps

Chapter Five: Pros and Cons of Canning and Consuming Canned Foods

Food preservation is very important, especially in today's world where food wastage is very rampant. Canning is one of the easiest and best ways to preserve food and prolong its shelf life. Here are some more reasons why you should consider canning:

1. You can capitalize on seasonal foods and flavors. Canning fresh ingredients that are widely available during their season will allow you to enjoy said flavor

Chapter Five: Pros & Cons of Canning

even when they are already out of season. You get the best nutrition and the best flavors all year long.

2. When you can your own food, you know what you are eating. You avoid all the pesticides and GMOs that come with processed or other store-brought food. You can grow your own fruits and vegetables or choose organic and sustainable products. You can control the amount of sugar or salt that you put in what you can. This way you have control over your choices and what you put inside your body.

3. By canning, you will save excess produce whether you have grown them at home or purchased them in the market. You can even ask your family members or friends for excess fruits or vegetables that you may can instead of them throwing it away. Eliminate waste and save on cost.

4. You can supplement your menu by growing and preserving your own food. What's more you can make your food as delicious as you want it to be.

5. You can support local and organic farmers. By buying organic produce, you are supporting small, local farmers and not commercial (pesticide-laden, GMO-smothered) produce by giant, industrialized farming companies.

6. You can enjoy different kinds of flavors that are not available in the supermarkets. You can look for lesser known varieties of fruits and vegetables, like black apples, watermelon radishes, or purple asparagus, can them and make them available in your home. You can experiment on different spices and herb combinations to make new sauces or condiments as well.

7. You can prove that the real flavor is on the inside and your food doesn't have to look perfect to taste just right. Even if you have damaged or bruised fruit in your pantry, you can use it to create a delicious jelly or jam. Irregularly shaped vegetables can be made into delicious pickles.

Chapter Five: Pros & Cons of Canning

8. Canning is like having your own time capsule in a pantry shelf. You can enjoy any fruit or vegetable throughout all the seasons!

9. You will feel pride and satisfaction with your endeavor. Not only did you eliminate waste, save money and produced something good and healthy to eat, you also increased in your skill and knowledge – and boost your self-confidence!

10. You can share the tradition of canning to the next generation. Teach your children, nieces or nephews the joys and importance of preserving food. Leave a good legacy by passing on your skills so that they can benefit from it in the future.

Canning food will not only allow you to enjoy it, but will also give you the opportunity to share the bounty with others. Share your jars of jellies, jams, pickles, condiments, and sauces with friends, family and neighbors. Who knows, you may even become an entrepreneur and earn a profit out

Chapter Five: Pros & Cons of Canning

of something that can start as a simple hobby or an advocacy.

Consuming Canned Foods

There is a shortage of safe, quality foods in many parts of the globe, even in places where there is bountiful harvest, when proper food preservation and storage is not done. Canning is a great technique that can guarantee that a wide selection of food can be accessed by people all over the world. Truth be told, all kinds of food can be found in a can nowadays! They can be shipped and stored to many different places and can be ready-to-eat or require minimal preparation.

It is truly healthy and important to eat more fruits and vegetables, but people question if it really matters a lot whether you prepare them from fresh ones or get them from a can.

Chapter Five: Pros & Cons of Canning

Here are some benefits of getting canned food as well as disadvantages or dangers associated with them:

Advantages of Consuming Canned Foods

- Canned foods are more affordable than most fresh foods. Even if you are not making your own canned foods, you can save on cost as canned fruits and vegetables are available all year round and are not affected by seasonal sale price. You can even buy canned fruit and vegetables in bulk when they are sold at a discount. If you have a tight budget, canned produce may be the best option.

- Canned foods are more convenient to prepare. They are easy to use when preparing meals as they are already sliced, peeled, pre-cooked and cut. You only need to re-heat them prior to eating. Remember not to overcook canned produce so that you don't lose more nutrients. In case you need to extend a recipe, you can easily add in canned veggies to serve more people. For example, a can of mixed vegetables or beans can make bigger casserole dishes or soups. When you get home from a busy day at work or school and you don't feel like preparing your food, you can still eat healthy by opening up canned produce for dinner. Not many people have the luxury of time to cook, and that makes canned products convenient.

- Canned foods have a long shelf life. You can stock up on canned produce without the worry of spoilage or wastage. This is very useful for -emergency situations.

- Canned foods don't easily spoil so you can eat fruits and vegetables that are not in season and not readily available in the market. Canned foods can be a source of essential nutrients and antioxidants. Even if it is a wide belief, canned fruits and vegetables are not inferior to fresh or frozen ones. Often, fresh produce lose their nutrients while they are being transferred from farm to store. Fruits and vegetables are canned immediately after harvest so their nutritional content is preserved.

Chapter Five: Pros & Cons of Canning

- Canned foods are a practical way to eat additional nutrient-dense foods. Even if vitamins B and C may be lost in the cutting, peeling and heating of canned foods, other nutritional levels will remain the same for a minimum of one to two years. The same can't be said of fresh fruits and vegetables. Antioxidants, beta carotene and lycopene are also enhanced during the canning process so you get more from canned berries carrots and tomatoes!

- Canned foods are better than not having any fruit or vegetable at all! There is still some goodness in the produce that is found in cans, and if you are not partial to or you don't have access to fresh produce, you can get them from canned ones.

- If you are canning your own food, you can avoid the extra salt, sugar or preservatives and have healthier options.

Chapter Five: Pros & Cons of Canning

Disadvantages of Consuming Canned Foods

- Some canned foods have high sugar or high salt content. Sugar or salt is usually added to canned foods to enhance flavor, appearance and texture. This does not always mean bad things for many people but it can cause a health risk for people who have diabetes, high blood pressure and other illnesses that can be aggravated by added chemicals.

- Some canned foods are loaded with preservatives/additives such as sulfites. Sulfites include sodium sulfite, potassium bisulfite and sulfur oxide. They prolong the shelf life of food but may cause adverse effects on health. Some people can be so badly affected by sulfites that they may experience reactions and need medical attention in as fast as a few hours after consumption.

- There may be traces of Bisphenol-A or BPA in some can linings that can transfer to the food you eat. BPA is associated with heart disease, diabetes and other health problems.

- While it is quite rare, some canned foods—that are not properly canned, especially if they are home canned—can be contaminated with deadly bacteria that cause botulism. Botulism can lead to paralysis or even death. If you are purchasing canned products, make sure they are not leaking, dented, cracked or bulging. Also, if the food inside the can or bottle smells off, it is likely spoiled. However, the risk of contamination in commercially canned goods is low.

- Some canned foods have fewer nutritional values. Even if canning sometimes increases the nutritional content of some foods, it does not happen to all foods. There are fruits and vegetables that become less nutritious after they have been canned, especially when they are peeled and they lose their fiber content. Vitamin C is also destroyed by heat during the canning process.

- There is lack of variety with canned foods. While you can a lot of fruits and vegetables, you can't can them all. And some of those that can be canned do not taste as good compared to when they are eaten fresh. For instance, you would be hard-pressed to find canned bananas.

- Canned food tastes canned, that is if you purchase canned foods that are not in bottles. Some canned fruits may taste sweeter because of added syrup or sugar, but there will always be the taste of can.

Health Risks

Botulism is one of the primary and very serious illnesses that one can get from eating canned food that is improperly processed. Signs and symptoms of botulism can appear within 12 – 36 hours after eating contaminated canned food. If you experience the following symptoms, make sure to get medical attention:

- Nausea
- Vomiting
- Dizziness
- Double vision
- Headache
- Fatigue
- Dryness in nose
- Dryness in throat

The symptoms can last for two hours to two weeks. Other symptoms last longer and severe cases of botulism can result in major health issues such as paralysis, respiratory failure, and death. People who have higher risk of grave effects on their health are people with weak immune system, children below 5 years old, pregnant women, and adults over 60 years.

Make the Right Choices

Canned, fresh, or frozen, you should always check the label and read the ingredient list of any food that you wish to consume. Not all canned foods have additional sugar, salt or chemical preservatives. It is wise to know what you put

Chapter Five: Pros & Cons of Canning

inside your body. For example, you are conscious about your salt intake then choose foods that have low sodium or are labeled with "no salt added". If you need to avoid sugar, get fruits that are canned in juice or water and avoid those that are canned in syrup. You can also drain and rinse canned food before consumption so you can reduce the sugar and salt content in them.

When fresh foods are available, you should always choose them. But when there is unavailability, it is not bad to make canned foods as an option for nutrition.

Chapter Five: Pros & Cons of Canning

Chapter Six: Possible Issues with Canned Foods: Causes and Solutions

As with all the other kinds of food preservation methods, there can be possible problems when it comes to canning foods. This chapter will discuss the causes of such potential issues as well as preventative measures to ensure that you can food that is safe to store and ear.

Liquid is lost in the glass jars during processing.

When you encounter this problem, do not try to replace the liquid inside. This is not necessarily a sign of spoilage. It can be caused by a number of factors.

Chapter Six: Possible Issues with Canned Foods

- Loss of liquid can happen as a result of a sudden lowering or pressure in the canner after the food is processed. To avoid this, you should not force the pressure down by running the canner over cold water, opening the vent too early, or putting the canner in a draft. The pressure should naturally drop to zero and does not require your intervention. You should wait for about ten minutes before you remove the weight and open the canner.

- Loss of liquid also occurs due to fluctuating pressures during the processing. Avoid this by making sure that constant temperature is maintained all throughout the process.

- Loss of liquid also happens when the air bubbles are not removed prior to processing. To remove them properly and avoid this problem, you can run a knife or a plastic spatula between the food and the jar before you place the lids.

Chapter Six: Possible Issues with Canned Foods

- There is loss of liquid when the seal is imperfect. Make sure you use new flat lids for your jars and that your lids have no flaws. Ring bands should have no dents, no rust and no bends. Ensure that lids are pretreated according to the manufacturer's instructions. You should also make sure that the sealing surface is wiped clean before the lid is applied.

- There is loss of liquid when ring bands are not tightened properly. While you should not overtighten the ring bands, you can apply fingertip-tight pressure over the lid.

- When you use boiling water technique and the jars are not covered with water, there will be loss of liquid. Make sure that there is an allowance of 1 to 2 inches of water during the process.

- If you are using starchy foods, there will be loos of liquid as these types of foods absorb water. Make sure

Chapter Six: Possible Issues with Canned Foods

that starchy foods are well rehydrated before you can them. Hot packs are used for starchy foods.

- When foods are packed too tightly, water boils over during the processing period and there is loss. Ensure the suitable headspace to avoid this.

Your finished product has a darker color at the top of the jar.

When your product has a darker color at the top of the jar, it doesn't mean it is spoiled. There are a number of reasons for this phenomenon:

- Oxidation happens when air is left inside the jar and this causes the darkening of color. To avoid oxidation, remove air bubbles prior to sealing and ensure correct headspace.

- When food is not processed with the appropriate period after the jars were filled and applied with lids,

Chapter Six: Possible Issues with Canned Foods

a darkening will occur. Observe the recommended processing time.

- When there is not enough syrup or liquid to cover all food products inside the jar, a darkening will occur. Foods should be completely soaked in syrup or water.

There are unattractive color changes in the product.

Sometimes, canned or bottled food can have undesirable color changes as a result of different elements:

- When food has contact with iron, copper or zinc through water or cooking utensils, these minerals can affect the color of the food. Make sure that you use soft water and use good quality cooking utensils free of these minerals.

- When you over-process the food, the color becomes unattractive. Carefully observe the correct procedures, canner operation and processing times per recipe.

Chapter Six: Possible Issues with Canned Foods

- When you use immature or overripe fruits and vegetables, you will have an ugly-colored product. Make sure to pick produce that are at the optimal age of maturity.

- Exposure to light can also cause changes in color. After processing, you should store canned or bottled foods in a dark, cool place.

- Some fruits or vegetables have natural yet harmless substances that can affect overall color of the product.

- There may also be a noticeable spoilage when you see unattractive color changes in your processed food. Dispose of it immediately.

The seal is imperfect.

When you discover that there is an imperfect seal, you should discard the food immediately.

Chapter Six: Possible Issues with Canned Foods

- Imperfect seals can be caused by cracks or chips in the sealing surface of your jar. Make sure that you check your jars before you use them and before you apply the lid.

- Imperfect seals are also caused by the failure to prepare flat lids correctly. Make sure that you follow manufacturer's instructions to avoid this from happening.

- When there are particles left on the mouth of the jar during sealing, you will have an imperfect seal. As you apply flat lids, use a clean, damp cloth so you can remove seasonings, seeds and other particles.

- Ring bands should always be in good condition because when you use bad ones, you will get an imperfect seal.

- Similarly, when you do not apply the right tightness to the ring bands you will have imperfect seals.

Chapter Six: Possible Issues with Canned Foods

- Make sure to use a jar lifter when you remove the jars from your canner. When you invert the jars after they have been processed or you lift them by the tops while they are hot, you can cause an imperfect seal. Jars should always be kept upright and using jar lifters will ensure that they are held just below the ring bands.

- When there is fat on the rim of the jar, you will have an imperfect seal. Before processing, trim out all the fat from meat and do not include any extra fat. Before sealing, wipe the rim of the jar.

The liquid is cloudy.

Cloudy liquid in your final product can be caused by many things. Often it can denote spoilage.

- Using starchy food or over-mature ones can cause a cloudy liquid in your jar. Choose products that are not immature and not too ripe. If you are going to can

Chapter Six: Possible Issues with Canned Foods

potatoes, fresh boiling water should be used and not the cooking liquid.

- Always use soft water so there won't be any minerals that will cause clouding.

- Always use refined salt, canning salt or pickling salt that have no additives. The additives can also cause clouding.

- When food is not processed according to the set time, there can be spoilage and it can be noticeable through a cloudy liquid.

There is presence of sediments.

Consider the following factors when you notice sediments in your processed jars:

- Starchy food can have sediments.

- Sediments can come from minerals found in water. Again, always use soft water.

Chapter Six: Possible Issues with Canned Foods

- Use salt without additives to avoid sedimentation.

- There is a natural yellow sediment when you can onions or green vegetables.

- There will be white crystal-like sediments when you can spinach

- There may also be spoilage if the food is processed inappropriately. Make sure to observe the right preparation and processing time.

- Some sediment may settle at the bottom of the jar. To minimize these sediments, you should strain the juice of the fruit before you can it. If you are going to can fruit juices, it should be shaken when consumed as a beverage.

There is spoilage of canned food.

Spoilage can be prevented. The reason why you are canning is to be able to preserve food and store it for a later

Chapter Six: Possible Issues with Canned Foods

time. But if you are not careful, all your hard work can go to waste.

- Spoilage after the canning procedure can happen when products are not selected well. When you use a poor quality of fruits, vegetables or meat to can, you may have problems when it comes to decomposition. Your products should be from a suitable variety and appropriately mature. Some produce should be canned immediately after being harvested.

- When you do not use the appropriate temperature for the type of food you are canning, spoilage can occur. For example, if you will can low acid foods using a boiling water method, you will surely face spoilage. When temperatures keep fluctuating, the processing will also not be appropriate.

- When you allow incorrect process time and pressure. Always follow instructions for canner operations and timing on recipes. You should always check the dial

Chapter Six: Possible Issues with Canned Foods

gauges on your canner so they will be accurate. Make sure that jars are not overfilled.

- When there are imperfect seals, spoilage is bound to happen. Wipe the jar rims before you close them and check the lids and jars before you use them for any signs of damage. Again, fill the jar appropriately.

Some food particles are floating.

When you can fruits, you will often notice that there will be some pieces that will float. These are normally okay.

- You can avoid floating fruit when you use ripe yet firm fruits. When fruit is lighter than the syrup that you use, they will float. You can use a light or medium syrup but never a heavy one.

- Heat the fruit before packing. This will ensure that there is no air trapped.

Chapter Six: Possible Issues with Canned Foods

- Make sure that you pack the fruit closely but not to the point of crushing them. Improper packing can result in floating. Additionally, remove all bubbles before you put the lid on. The liquid should cover all the food pieces entirely.

The flavor of the final product is poor.

Reasons for poor flavor can be because of improper storage, poor quality of fruit or vegetable used and excessive use of water during extraction of fruit juice.

- Always store your jars in dark, dry and cool places to preserve the flavor.

- Only can good quality food. Avoid overripe, immature and inferior quality fruits or vegetables.

- Always follow instructions especially the amount of water you should use. For instance, you should not add water to tomatoes.

Chapter Six: Possible Issues with Canned Foods

Chapter Seven: Simple Home Canning Recipes

Home canning is becoming popular again and for good reason! Preserving food at the height of it freshness and nutritional peak serves so much purpose — creating fabulous recipes, sharing your bounty, avoiding wastage, saving costs and even tempting choosy kids. Here is a compilation of easy-to-do jams, pickles, and sauces that you can make at home. You won't find any canning recipes for meat, poultry and seafood in this chapter.

Chapter Seven: Simple Home Canning Recipes

Common Canning Recipes

As a beginner, you ought to start with the simple recipes. Before you start cooking, you need to prepare the things you will be using:

- water bath canner or pressure canner
- canning jars
- canning seals and rings
- jar lifter and canning funnel
- large pot or blancher
- bowls
- large spoons
- whisk
- ladle
- slotted spoons
- stock pots
- plastic spatula or sharp knife
- towels and dish cloths
- fruit peeler, if necessary

Chapter Seven: Simple Home Canning Recipes

Spaghetti Sauce

Ingredients	Measurement
Tomatoes	25 pounds
Green peppers	4, big and seeded
White Onions	4, big and cut into wedges
Garlic	4 cloves
Tomato Paste	2 12-oz cans
Canola Oil	1 cup
Sugar	2/3 cup
Salt	¼ cup
Dried Oregano	4 teaspoons
Dried Basil	2 teaspoons
Dried Parsley	2 teaspoons
Bay leaves	2 pieces
Worcestershire Sauce	2 teaspoons
Lemon Juice	1 cup + 1 teaspoon

You will need nine 1-quart jars.

Chapter Seven: Simple Home Canning Recipes

How to Prepare

1. Bring water to a boil.

2. Use a slotted spoon to put the tomatoes one by one in boiling water for about 30 to 60 seconds.

3. Remove the tomatoes from the boiling water and plunge them immediately into ice water.

4. Peel and cut them in quarters and put them in a stock pot.

5. Using a food processor, pulse the onions and green peppers in batches so that they will be finely chopped. Then add them to the stock pot.

6. Add water and the other 11 ingredients to the stockpot. Then bring it to boil.

Chapter Seven: Simple Home Canning Recipes

7. Once the mixture boils, reduce the heat and allow it to simmer without a cover for about 4 to 5 hours. Don't forget to stir the mixture occasionally.

8. Remove the bay leaves from the mixture.

9. Put two tablespoons of lemon juice in each of the nine hot one-quart jars.

10. Pour the hot mixture into the jars, with a half inch headspace.

11. Remove the bubbles.

12. Make sure you wipe the rims clean before you put the center lids on and screw the band rings tight.

13. Put the jars into your canner that has simmering water, making sure that there is enough water to cover the jars.

14. Bring the water to a boil and process the jars for 40 minutes. The 40-minute processing time is based on

altitude of 1,000 feet or less. Add five minutes for altitudes of 3,000 feet, 10 minutes for 6,000 feet, 15 minutes for 8,000 feet and 20 minutes for 10,000 feet.

15. Remove the jars from the canner and allow it to cool naturally on cooling racks or towels.

Pesto Sauce

Have extra basil? Then you can put it to good use—make pesto sauce!

Ingredients	Measurement
Fresh Basil	2 cups
Extra Virgin Olive Oil	½ cup
Parmesan Cheese	½ cup, grated
Pine nuts	1/3 cup
Garlic	2 cloves, minced
Salt	¼ teaspoon
Black Pepper	¼ teaspoon, ground

You will need one pint jar.

Chapter Seven: Simple Home Canning Recipes

How to Prepare

1. Rinse the basil leaves and pat them dry.

2. Pulse the leaves and the pine nuts in a food processor until fully crushed.

3. Add the olive oil into the food processor and blend until the mixture becomes smooth.

4. Add the parmesan cheese and pulse a few times.

5. Make sure you scrape of any mixture or ingredient that has found its way to the side of the food processor.

6. Add one minced garlic clove to the mixture and pulse again. If you prefer more of the garlic taste, add another clove.

7. Add the pepper and salt and pulse again.

8. Put the pesto in a clean, sterilized pint jar. You will notice a thin layer of olive oil at the top of your mixture.

9. Put the lid on the jar and refrigerate it.

10. You don't have to process the pesto sauce in a boiling water canner. Some ingredients in the mixture can allow the bacteria that cause botulism to grow when they are heated. According to the Nacional Center for Home Food Preservation, pesto can be stored for a long time. To preserve it, you can store it in containers or freezer bags and put them in the freezer until use.

Super Cherry Jam

Don't be limited to pineapple and strawberry jams, you can also create and enjoy your own cherry jam.

Ingredients	Measurement
Tart Cherries	2 ½ pounds, fresh and pitted

Chapter Seven: Simple Home Canning Recipes

Powdered Fruit

Pectin	1 pack (1 ¾ oz)
Sugar	4 ¾ cups
Butter	½ teaspoon

You will need six half-pint jars.

How to Prepare

1. Process cherries in a food processor until they are finely chopped.

2. Transfer processed cherries on a Dutch oven and add in butter and pectin.

3. Put the heat on to high and bring the mixture to a full boil while stirring continuously, for a five minutes.

4. Lower the heat a little and add in the sugar, then heat it up again to full rolling boil for about a minute.

5. Remove the mixture from heat.

Chapter Seven: Simple Home Canning Recipes

6. Make sure you skim off the foam.

7. Pour the cherry mixture into six half-pint jars that have been sterilized.

8. Make sure there is a quarter inch of headspace.

9. Remove air bubbles.

10. Wipe the rims clean and put on the lids and screw bands

11. Put the jars in the canner with simmering water and boil for 5 minutes.

12. Remove the jars from the canner and allow to cool naturally on cooling racks or towels.

Yummy Fig Jam

Figs make the best jams and they are perfect for your next breakfast toast.

Chapter Seven: Simple Home Canning Recipes

Ingredients	Measurement
Figs	2 pounds, fresh
Sugar	¼ cup
Lemon juice	½ lemon
Cinnamon	a dash

*You will need six half-pint jars.

How to Prepare

1. Wash the figs and cut them in quarters.

2. Put them in a pan with the ¼ cup of sugar.

3. Cook over low heart. The figs will break down. You can also use a blender to create a fig puree.

4. As the mixture is heated, it will have a darker color and become smoother. Continue stirring and heating.

5. Once the fig mixture thickens you will notice that it detaches from the sides of the pan. To test the thickness,

Chapter Seven: Simple Home Canning Recipes

use a spatula to scrape over the bottom of the pan and when the jam does not slide back to the cleared area again, it is thick enough.

6. Take it out of the heat and add in the cinnamon and lemon juice

7. Make sure there is a quarter inch of headspace.

8. Remove air bubbles.

9. Clean the rims by wiping them then put on the lids and screw bands.

10. Put the jars in the canner with simmering water and boil for 5 minutes.

11. Remove the jars from the canner and allow to cool naturally on cooling racks or towels.

Chapter Seven: Simple Home Canning Recipes

Super Apple Pie Filling

Making this recipe will allow you to have dessert already half-ready. You can have apple pie anytime of the year and not just on Thanksgiving!

Ingredients	**Measurement**
Apples	6 quarts, sliced
Sugar	5 cups
Clear Jelly	1 cup
Cinnamon	1 teaspoon
Nutmeg	1 teaspoon
Salt	2 teaspoons
Water	10 cups
Lemon Juice	3 tablespoons

How to Prepare

1. Wash, peel and core the apples before slicing them. You may use an apple corer, peeler and slicer if you prefer thinly sliced apples, as well as to shorten the preparation time.

Chapter Seven: Simple Home Canning Recipes

2. To make the thickener or syrup you have to combine clear gel, sugar, lemon juice, cinnamon and nutmeg.

3. Stir the thickener into ten cups of water and heat it up. Stir the mixture until it is thick and bubbly.

For raw packing apples, put them in a treatment solution (water with ascorbic acid) or light syrup (dissolve 2 cups sugar in 1 quart of water) after peeling to prevent browning. You need to prepare enough apples that can fill one jar at a time. Then pour hot syrup over it. Use a spatula to remove air bubbles. And fill the jar with syrup with a 1-inch headspace. Wipe the rims clean and place the lids. Do it again until you use all the apples.

However, hot pack is highly recommended. Prepare all the apples and put them in a large pot of hot water to boil for a minute. Drain. Then combine the apple with thickened mixture. Use a spatula to remove air bubbles. And fill the jar with syrup with a 1-inch headspace. Wipe the rims clean and place the lids.

4. Put the jars in the canner with simmering water and boil. Processing time is 25 minutes.

5. Remove the jars from the canner and allow to cool naturally on cooling racks or towels.

Canned Carrots

You can use canned carrots as an ingredient for soup or stew, or you can have it for a snack by adding butter and a bit of cinnamon. You need a pressure canner because carrots are low acid vegetables.

Tip: use a crinkle cutter when you slice your carrots so they look attractive. You can also prepare sweet syrup as a treat.

Ingredients	Measurement
Carrots	
Canning Salt optional	
Brown sugar	2 cups
Water	2 cups
Orange juice	1 cup

Chapter Seven: Simple Home Canning Recipes

How to Prepare

1. Wash and peel carrots.

2. Cut the carrots to the desired size and length. It is ideal to not cut the carrots too small as they will become mushy when pressure canned. You can also leave them whole if you are using baby carrots.

3. You can hot pack or raw pack carrots. For hot packs, simmer carrots slices for 5 minutes and put them in hot jars with a 1-inch headspace. For raw packing, put carrots directly into hot jars with 1-inch headspace.

4. Put boiling water in the jars to cover the carrots, with 1-inch headspace.

5. Add canning salt if you like: ½ teaspoon per pint.

6. Make sure you release any bubbles using a plastic spatula or knife.

7. Put the jars into your canner that has simmering water, making sure that there is enough water to cover the jars.

8. Bring the water to a boil and process the jars for 40 minutes. The 40-minute processing time is based on altitude of 1,000 feet or less. Add five minutes for altitudes of 3,000 feet, 10 minutes for 6,000 feet, 15 minutes for 8,000 feet and 20 minutes for 10,000 feet.

9. Remove the jars from the canner and allow to cool naturally on cooling racks or towels.

* To make sweet syrup, heat brown sugar and orange juice together—use it in place of plain water. Pour over the carrots with 1-inch headspace. Same processing instructions.

Mild Tomato Salsa

Everyone loves salsa and it is good to always have a jar handy. Here is a recipe for a lazy day salsa that you can store for a long time.

Chapter Seven: Simple Home Canning Recipes

Ingredients	Measurement
Tomatoes	10 ½ pounds, peeled and quartered
Green Peppers	4, medium, chopped
Sweet Red Pepper	1, chopped
Celery	1 rib, chopped
Garlic	15 cloves, minced
Jalapeño peppers	4 pieces, seeded and chopped
White Onions	3 large, chopped
Tomato Paste	2 12-oz cans
Canning Salt	¼ cup
Sugar	½ cup
Hot Pepper Sauce	¼ to ½ teaspoon
White Vinegar	1/3 cup

*You will need ten one-pint jars.

How to Prepare

1. Cook tomatoes over medium heat in a stockpot, without a cover, for 20 minutes. Drain and reserve 2 cups of the tomato liquid.

2. Put the tomatoes back in the pot and stir in the onions, peppers, sugar, vinegar, garlic, jalapeño, hot pepper sauce, 2 cups of tomato liquid, celery, and tomato paste.

3. Bring the mixture to a boil then simmer for an hour, with frequent stirring.

4. Put the hot mixture in sterilized jars with 1 inch headspace.

5. Remove all the air bubbles.

6. Clean the rims by wiping them then put on the lids and screw bands.

7. Put the jars in the canner with simmering water and process for 20 minutes.

8. Remove the jars from the canner and allow to cool naturally on cooling racks or towels.

Chapter Seven: Simple Home Canning Recipes

Strawberry Basil Jam

Don't be limited to pineapple and strawberry jams, you can also create and enjoy your own cherry jam.

Ingredients	Measurement
Strawberries	3 pounds or 5 cups, crushed
Powdered Fruit Pectin	1 pack (1 ¾ oz)
Sugar	7 cups
Butter	1 teaspoon
Fresh basil	½ cup, minced

*You will need nine half-pint jars.

How to Prepare

1. Put strawberries on a Dutch oven and add in butter and pectin.

2. Put the heat on to high and bring the mixture to a full boil while stirring continuously, for a five minutes.

3. Lower the heat a little and add in the sugar, then heat it up again to full rolling boil for about a minute. Stir in the minced basil leaves.

4. Remove the mixture from heat.

5. Make sure you skim off the foam.

6. Pour the cherry mixture into six half-pint jars that have been sterilized.

7. Make sure there is a quarter inch of headspace.

8. Remove air bubbles.

9. Wipe the rims clean and put on the lids and screw bands

10. Put the jars in the canner with simmering water and boil for 5 minutes.

11. Remove the jars from the canner and allow to cool naturally on cooling racks or towels.

Chapter Seven: Simple Home Canning Recipes

Pickled Strawberries (and Yoghurt Parfait)

Did you know you can pickle strawberries so that you don't have to wait for strawberry season to enjoy them? You can also enjoy pickled strawberries by serving them in yoghurt parfait. Try this recipe today!

Tips:

- Use mason jars so you will be successful with acidic brine.
- For the brine, completely dissolve the salt and sugar in the liquid before pouring it on the berries.
- Strawberries have the tendency to float so make sure you pack them tightly.
- You can use the brine that is left after you use up your first jar of pickled strawberry.
- Pickled strawberries can also be served with strawberry shortcake, salads, pizza, martinis and margaritas.

Chapter Seven: Simple Home Canning Recipes

For Pickled Strawberries

Ingredients	Measurement
Strawberries	1 pound, fresh and hulled
Champagne vinegar	1 cup
Water	½ cup
Granulated Sugar	½ to ¾ cup
Kosher salt	1 tablespoon

You will need nine half-pint jars.

How to Prepare

1. Wash the strawberries, and cut them in halves or quarters.
2. In a medium sized sauce pan, put water, vinegar, sugar and salt and heat on medium. Stir to dissolve the salt and sugar.
3. Raw pack the strawberries in the sterilized jars.
4. Once the salt and sugar have dissolved completely, turn the heat off and pour the mixture onto the jars to cover the strawberries, with 1 inch headspace.

Chapter Seven: Simple Home Canning Recipes

5. Seal the jar with the lid tightly.
6. The pickled strawberries will be ready after an hour.
7. You can store the pickles in a refrigerator for up to 5 days only

For Yogurt Parfait

Ingredients	Measurement
Vanilla Greek Yogurt	2 cups, nonfat
Granola	½ cup
Pickled Strawberries	2 cups

How to Prepare (for two highball glasses)

1. Drain the pickled strawberries and Scoop up ¼ of it (or half cup) on a highball glass.
2. Top the strawberries with half a cup of nonfat Greek yoghurt.
3. Repeat making layers.
4. Top each glass with ¼ cup granola.
5. Serve the parfait immediately.

Jalapeño Cucumber Dill Pickles

Are you game for some spicy pickles? Then this tangy mix is the tickle your fancy.

Ingredients	Measurement
Pickling Cucumbers	3 pounds
White onion	1, small and sliced
Fresh Dill	¼ cup fresh and snipped
Jalapeño peppers	2 pieces, seeded and sliced
Garlic	3 cloves, minced
Water	2 ½ cups
Cider vinegar	2 ½ cups
Canning salt	1/3 cup
Sugar	1/3 cup

How to Prepare

1. Wash and cut the cucumber lengthwise, making four spears.
2. Combine the sliced cucumbers with the dill, onion, garlic and jalapeños in a bowl.

Chapter Seven: Simple Home Canning Recipes

3. On a saucepan, put the water, vinegar, sugar and salt and bring the mixture to a boil, until the sugar and salt are completely dissolved.
4. Put the cucumber mixture in hot, sterilized jars and pour over the solution, enough to cover the vegetables.
5. Cover the jar tightly and refrigerate for a minimum of 24 hours.
6. You can store the jalapeño cucumber dill pickles for about two months.

Holiday Pepper Jelly

Red and green pepper jelly is a very delectable appetizer, especially when served over cream cheese. Canned pepper jelly also makes for great gifts during holidays or if you are planning a kitchen basket present. Make sure you have a couple of jars at home so that you don't have to worry about serving something fancy when you have unexpected guests.

Chapter Seven: Simple Home Canning Recipes

Ingredients	Measurement
Green Bell Peppers	1 cup, finely chopped
Red Bell Peppers	1 cup, finely chopped
Jalapeño peppers	2 pieces, seeded and minced
Cider vinegar	1 ½ cups
Hot pepper sauce	¼ teaspoon
Canning salt	1/3 cup
Sugar	6 ½ cups
Liquid pectin	2 3oz-pouches

You need five 8oz jars.

How to Prepare

1. Combine the peppers—green bell peppers, red bell peppers, and jalapeño peppers—with vinegar, sugar and hot pepper sauce in a big, heavy-bottomed pot. Over medium heating, bring the mixture to a boil while stirring continuously.
2. After boiling, reduce the heat and simmer for five minutes.
3. Remove from heat and allow to stand for about 20 minutes, stirring sporadically.

4. Put back over high heat and bring to a full rolling boil.
5. Mix the liquid pectin and let boil for a minute, stirring continually.
6. Remove from heat.
7. Take out any foam.
8. Stir the mixture for about 5 to 8 minutes so that the peppers won't float.
9. Pour the mixture into prepared, sterilized jars with a ¼ inch headspace.
10. Wipe the rims clean and put on the lids and screw bands.
11. Put the jars in the canner with simmering water and process for 10 minutes.
12. Remove the jars from the canner and allow to cool naturally on cooling racks or towels.
13. Let the jars rest in room temperature until the jelly sets.
14. Unsealed jars should be refrigerated and used within 3 weeks.
15. In order to test for floating peppers, fill one jar first then let it rest for a minute. If peppers will

float, then return the mixture to the pot and stir some more. Pour mixture in a new, sterilized jar.

There are so many canning recipes to make using fruits and vegetables. But if you are a beginner, you should exercise caution. Use tested recipes first and do not try to experiment, especially when it comes to processing. Following the requirements and procedures will ensure that the food you are canning is safe to eat. Sure you want to make something that is flavorful and appealing to the eyes, but your number one goal should be food safety.

Most recipes that you find in published books or other reputable sources may look easy to follow, but in reality they also closely follow USDA standards. Follow them and refrain from making even the most minor variations when you are only just starting to can. When you already have advanced knowledge as well as experience in canning foods, then you can create your own recipes, have your own recipes lab-tested and share them with the world. Oh what an adventure that would be!

Chapter Seven: Simple Home Canning Recipes

Conclusion

Now that you have learned the basics of canning as food preservation and storage, you can put the knowledge to good use. It is a fun and economical way to get the most of fresh fruits and vegetables, making them accessible all year round.

The consumption of canned goods may still be up for debate due to many factors, but the fact that canning is a great way to preserve the quality and lifespan of food cannot be minimized.

Canning is an amazing way to support a sustainable lifestyle: you can reuse tools (mason jars), reduce food waste, avoid packaging waste and maintain shelf stability. Home canning will give you the power to control your diet and free you from your dependence on store-bought food. More importantly, canning will give you a sense of accountability. You will find it hard to toss a leftover personally made jam into the garbage bin compared to throwing away something

Chapter Seven: Simple Home Canning Recipes

that you just bought from the grocery—it's something YOU made!

Lastly, even as canning is economical and enjoyable, it is also an activity that will allow you to practice mindfulness. Not surprisingly, you will find yourself taking time to think about the jam you just spread or the sauce you just ate. You will remember how you lovingly and carefully crafted it and you will enjoy it even more. You will look back and look ahead—how can you improve your recipe? How often should you prepare canned foods? Who can you share it with?

Photo Credits

Page 1 Photo by user PhotoMIX-Company via Pixabay.com,

https://pixabay.com/en/pickled-cucumbers-homemade-preserves-1520638/

Page 5 Photo by user ulleo via Pixabay.com,

https://pixabay.com/en/beans-lenses-quail-beans-legumes-2014062/

Page 18 Photo by user M Prince Photography via Flickr.com,

https://www.flickr.com/photos/coffeegeeker/35042659843/

Page 31 Photo by user fshnextension via Pixabay.com,

https://pixabay.com/en/mason-jars-dehydrated-fruit-oranges-2742757/

Page 51 Photo by user congerdesign via Pixabay.com,

https://pixabay.com/en/tomatoes-sun-dried-tomatoes-oil-2500856/

Page 73 Photo by user congerdesign via Pixabay.com,

https://pixabay.com/en/cucumbers-pickle-jar-preserves-886036/

Page 87 Photo by user MissCaraReads via Pixabay.com,

https://pixabay.com/en/jam-jelly-jar-food-homemade-fruit-2091026/

Page 101 Photo by user labenord via Pixabay.com,

https://pixabay.com/en/jams-marmalades-farmers-market-997593/

References

"Canning Basics for Preserving Food" – Canning – Food – Recipes.com

http://www.canning-food-recipes.com/canning.htm

"The 5 Best Ways to Preserve Food" – CanadianLiving.com

http://www.canadianliving.com/food/food-tips/article/the-5-best-ways-to-preserve-food

"How to Preserve Food: Methods and Techniques" – FineDiningLovers.com

https://www.finedininglovers.com/blog/food-drinks/how-to-preserve-food-techniques/

"Common Methods of Food Preservation" – TheSpruceEats.com

https://www.thespruceeats.com/methods-of-food-preservation-1328477

"12 Food Preservation Methods to Make Your Food & Harvest Last Longer" – MorningChores.com

https://morningchores.com/food-preservation-methods/

"Food Preservation" – Encyclopedia.com

https://www.encyclopedia.com/sports-and-everyday-life/food-and-drink/food-and-cooking/food-preservation

"Why Can't I Can My Own Recipe at Home" – PickYourOwn.org

http://pickyourown.org/canning_my_own_recipe.php

"Top 10 Canning Recipes" – TasteofHome.com

https://www.tasteofhome.com/collection/top-10-canning-recipes/view-all/

"Our favorite Canning Recipes" – TasteofHome.com

https://www.tasteofhome.com/collection/favorite-canning-recipes/view-all/

"Canning Made Easy" – Parents.com

https://www.parents.com/recipes/tips/canning-made-easy

"Home Canning Meat Poultry, Red Seafood" – North Dakota State University

https://www.ag.ndsu.edu/publications/food-nutrition/home-canning-meat-poultry-red-meats-game-and-seafood

"29 Smart and Easy Tips to Reduce Food Waste" – Greatist.com

https://greatist.com/health/how-to-ways-reduce-food-waste

"Food Drying" – Wikipedia.org

https://en.wikipedia.org/wiki/Food_drying

"Storing food safely" – NIDirect.gov.uk

https://www.nidirect.gov.uk/articles/storing-food-safely

"Safe Food Storage" – Canada.ca

https://www.canada.ca/en/health-canada/services/general-food-safety-tips/safe-food-storage.html

"The Disadvantages of Canned Foods" – Livestrong.com

https://www.livestrong.com/article/465106-the-disadvantages-of-canned-foods/

"How Do I Can Fruits?" National Center for Home Food Preservation

https://nchfp.uga.edu/how/can2_fruit.html

"Storing & Preserving: Keeping Food Safe At Home" – Minnesota Department of Health

http://www.health.state.mn.us/foodsafety/store/index.html

www.ingramcontent.com/pod-product-compliance
Lightning Source LLC
LaVergne TN
LVHW051839080426
835512LV00018B/2960